BEETLES
of Australia

T0342941

Paul Zborowski

First published in 2024 by Reed New Holland Publishers
Sydney

Level 1, 178 Fox Valley Road, Wahroonga, NSW 2076, Australia

newhollandpublishers.com

A record of this book is held at the National Library of Australia.

ISBN 978 1 76079 611 2

Managing Director: Fiona Schultz
Publisher and Project Editor: Simon Papps
Designer: Andrew Davies
Production Director: Arlene Gippert

Printed in China

10 9 8 7 6 5 4 3 2 1

Keep up with Reed New Holland
and New Holland Publishers

ReedNewHolland
@ReedNewHolland

Front cover image: Flower Chafer, *Ischiopsopha* sp.

Page 1: Christmas Beetle, *Anoplognathus rugosus,* family/subfamily Scarabaeidae-Retulinae.

Page 19: Jewel Beetle, family Buprestidae.

Page 20: Leaf Beetle, *Paropsisterna nobilitata,* family Chrysomelidae.

Back cover image: Soft-winged Flower Beetle, *Dicranolaius* sp.

CONTENTS

Introduction

What is a beetle...6

Evolution...9

Life cycle 10

Habits 14

Classification 15

How to use this book..17

THE BEETLES

CARABIDAE – Ground Beetles 21

DYTISCIDAE – Diving Beetles 29

GYRINIDAE – Whirligig Beetles 32

HYDROPHILIDAE – Water Beetles 35

HISTERIDAE – Hister Beetles 38

LEIODIDAE – Small Fungus Beetles 39

SILPHIDAE – Carrion or Burying Beetles..............40

STAPHYLINIDAE – Rove Beetles 41

LUCANIDAE – Stag Beetles 45

PASSALIDAE – Passalid or Bess Beetles 50

TROGIDAE – Hide Beetles 51

GEOTRUPIDAE – Geotrupid Beetles....................52

HYBOSORIDAE – Scavenger Scarab Beetles 53

SCARABAEIDAE – Scarab Beetles, including Dung Beetles,
  Christmas Beetles and Chafers 54

  Retulinae – Christmas Beetles 54

  Scarabaeinae and Aphodiinae – Dung Beetles.................... 58

  Cetoniinae – Flower Chafers.. 61

  Melolonthinae – Chafers 65

  Dynastinae – Rhinoceros and Elephant Beetles................. 68

RHIPICERIDAE – Fan Beetles 70

BUPRESTIDAE – Jewel Beetles 71

ELATERIDAE – Click Beetles 79

LYCIDAE – Net-winged Beetles... 82

LAMPYRIDAE – Fireflies 84

CANTHARIDAE – Soldier Beetles 85

DERMESTIDAE – Dermestid, Carpet and Museum Beetles 87

BOSTRICHIDAE – Auger Beetles, Shothole Borers 89

LYMEXILIDAE – Ship-timber Beetles 90

CLERIDAE – Checkered Beetles 91

MELYRIDAE – Soft-winged Flower Beetles 95

NITIDULIDAE – Sap Beetles 98

SILVANIDAE – Silvanid Beetles... 100

CUCUJIDAE – Flat Bark Beetles 101

EROTYLIDAE – Pleasing Fungus Beetles.............................. 102

ENDOMYCHIDAE – Handsome Fungus Beetles....................... 104

COCCINELLIDAE – Ladybirds...105

MORDELLIDAE – Pin-tail or Tumbling Flower Beetles,
    Fish Beetles...111

RHIPIPHORIDAE – Wedge-shaped Beetles............................112

TENEBRIONIDAE – Darkling Beetles....................................114

OEDEMERIDAE – False Blister Beetles.................................124

MELOIDAE – Oil Beetles, Blister Beetles..............................125

ANTHICIDAE – Ant Beetles..127

CERAMBYCIDAE – Longicorn Beetles, Longhorn Beetles...........129

CHRYSOMELIDAE – Leaf Beetles..146

    Chrysomelinae...146

    Cassidinae..155

    Eumolpinae...158

    Cryptocephalinae 160

    Galerucinae..162

CURCULIONIDAE – Weevils..164

BRENTIDAE – Straight-snouted Weevils................................178

ATTELABIDAE – Leaf-rolling Weevils....................................181

ANTHRIBIDAE – Fungus Weevils...182

BELIDAE – Belid Weevils..184

Glossary 186

Further reading...187

Index 188

INTRODUCTION

What is a beetle

Like all insects, beetles have a head with antennae and various mouthparts, a thorax with three pairs of legs and usually wings, and an abdomen with the reproductive organs. Beetles belong to the insect order Coleoptera. Orders are higher-level classification groups, for example all flies are in the order Diptera, and all butterflies and moths are in the order Lepidoptera. The name Coleoptera describes a chief characteristic of beetles. It is

A beetle in the family **Rhipiphoridae** about to take off, showing the upper forewings, the elytra, in the open position, and the soft flying wings they protect spread out for flight.

composed of two old Greek words: *koleos*, meaning 'sheath or shield', and *pteron*, meaning 'wing'. Beetles have their upper forewings hardened into wing cases, called elytra. These hide the soft flying wings and the abdomen, protecting them from damage.

The bugs, order Hemiptera, and cockroaches, order Blattodea, also have hardened forewings, but their wings usually overlap, often exposing parts of the hindwings, whereas beetle forewing cases always meet in a straight middle line, and do not expose any part of the hindwings. This tough exterior is one reason for the amazing

A typical Shield Bug, family **Pentatomidae**, showing the cross-over wing cases, which expose part of the flying wings – the black triangle at the bottom.

proliferation and diversity of beetles. Current estimates are that about 1.5 million species exist worldwide, with more than 420,000 so far named. That is over 40 per cent of all insects. In Australia, about 25,000 beetle species are named. They have chewing, sideways-acting, mandible-type mouthparts (whereas bugs have sucking, proboscis-type mouthparts). Beetle antennae have a large variety of shapes, and can be very short or several times as long as the beetle itself, but all usually have 11 segments.

The beetles in the order Coleoptera include the largest, heaviest and smallest insect species in the world. The South American Hercules Beetle *Dynastes hercules* and the longicorn *Titanus*

Like all insects, beetle mandibles work sideways, not up and down, and are heavily sclerotised, or toughened. This Longicorn Beetle from the genus *Batocera* uses them to bite through bark.

giganteus can attain a length of 170mm. The heaviest are the Goliath Beetles from Africa, which can weigh more than 100g, while the smallest is a Feather-winged Beetle, *Scydosella* sp, at just 0.3mm, which is smaller than some single-celled amoeba.

One of Australia's largest beetles is this Ground Beetle, *Mecynognathus daemeli*, from Cape York Peninsula, Qld, which can reach 75mm. It is a formidable hunter.

Evolution

The earliest known recognisable beetle fossils are 295 million years old. Dinosaurs were around until 65 million years ago. More modern beetle groups, including recognisable beetle families that are still around today, appeared about 200 million years ago. The youngest lineages are in the group called Phytophaga that includes the Leaf Beetles, Longicorn Beetles and Weevils, which originate from around 180 million years ago.

Life cycle

Beetles belong to the insect groups which undergo full metamorphosis, also known as a complete life cycle. This means they start with an egg, progress to a larva, which then undergoes a pupa stage, and emerges as the final reproductive adult stage. This most often means that the larvae and the adults have different life habits. Like all insects, the outer 'skin' is the skeleton, called an exoskeleton, made of a very tough waterproof substance called chitin. To grow, the larvae sheds its outer 'skin' in several stages, each one having a larger skin to grow into. Adult beetles do not grow. They are the final stage, which has reproductive organs and usually wings, and has the job of mating and making the next generation. The larvae have many shapes, from caterpillar-like, to fat grubs, or underwater hunters. The head is heavily 'sclerotised' or toughened compared to other caterpillar-like larvae. They have

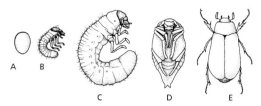

Stages in the complete metamorphosis life cycle, illustrated by a beetle in the family Scarabaeidae: (A) egg; (B) early larval stage; (C) final larval stage; (D) the stationary pupa showing developing adult characteristics, like wing sheaths; (E) the winged adult or imago.

A Leaf Beetle, *Paropsis* sp, **Chrysomelidae**, laying rows of eggs which will hatch into larvae that eat these leaves.

three pairs of usually short legs, and no extra prolegs along the abdomen, as in butterflies and moths. The pupal stage is mostly hidden, in the ground, or in wood, with a few leaf feeders having exposed pupa.

The life-cycle duration is dependent on many factors such as climate and quality of food, with the adult stage lasting from weeks to months, while the larva lasts from days to several years.

The life cycle of a Rose Chafer beetle, **Scarabaeidae – Cetoniinae**, showing an early- and late-stage larva, a pupa, and the adult.

The 'mealworms' that pet shops breed to feed pets, from birds to bats to reptiles, are actually the larvae of a Darkling Beetle, *Tenebrio molitor*. See family **Tenebrionidae** (page 114).

Most beetle larvae are solitary, but some, such as these Leaf Beetles, **Chrysomelidae**, live a gregarious life, stripping the surface of this leaf.

A beetle pupa often shows features of the adult to come. Here a Stag Beetle pupa already has the large mandibles of the adult male Stag Beetle.

Habits

There is almost no limit to the habits that beetles have adapted to. Every natural habitat has some or lots of beetle groups utilising it. Underwater hunters and scavengers; ground hunters; ground

The antennae of most insects are their organs of smell. Apart from finding food sources, the most important function is to pick up, and home in on, the pheromone scents created by the opposite sex. The **Callirhipidae** family has extra surface area on their fan-like antennae.

scavengers; leaf eaters; wood borers; tree-root eaters; dead-things eaters; pollen eaters; fruit eaters; seed eaters; fungus eaters; parasites, and more. Each of the 170 plus world families of beetles will have its speciality. The same diversity extends to where they live. While the majority of species are found in the wetter parts of the world, especially in rainforests, beetles are also very well adapted to deserts. Many beetle adults are only active at night, with notable exceptions being the Leaf Beetles (family **Chrysomelidae**), which feed exposed on leaves all day. Most families have fully formed flying hindwings, and the sexes find each other by flying towards species-specific 'find me' pheromone scents.

Classification

All beetles belong to the insect order Coleoptera. This is divided into four suborders. The Myxophaga, with only two species, and the Archostemata, with 10 species, are very unlikely to be seen and are not illustrated here. The Adephaga and the larger Polyphaga hold the rest. The number of named beetles in the world exceeds 420,000, in 174 families – the level at which, for instance, all ladybirds are in one family. Australia has about 25,000 named species in 117 families. Taking into account known, but not yet named species, and estimating the numbers awaiting discovery, the real Australian species number is at least 50,000.

Families are divided into genera, of which Australia has more than 3,300. And genera have species, from one to many. For instance, all ladybirds are in the family **Coccinellidae**. In this, the genus *Harmonia* has five species. One species in this genus is

The majority of beetle species are smaller than 10mm long, and often live hidden or nocturnal lives. However when a super resource, such as the *Angophora* flower nectar, presents itself, they can appear in mobs. In this image three different species of Rose Chafers are having a gluttonous time. **Scarabaeidae – Cetoniinae.**

Harmonia conformis, the Common Spotted Ladybird (see page 105). Family names all end in 'idae' and subfamily names end in 'inae'. Families are often presented in bold text, while genus and species names are always presented in italics.

A high percentage of the species numbers are concentrated in several very large families. The weevils, family **Curculionidae**, are the most diverse family of insects in the world, with more than 6,000 species in Australia alone. Leaf Beetles, **Chrysomelidae**, and Scarab Beetles, **Scarabaeidae**, have about 4,000 each, and the Ground Beetles, **Carabidae**, have around 3,000 species.

Taxonomy is an evolving science, and sometimes species are rearranged into a different family or genera, or a large genus is split up. This can mean that older books present the same species by a different name. In these cases, this book offers both the new and the old name.

How to use this book

The guide uses images of beetles taken in their natural surroundings, doing what they do. It is not always able to accurately identify each beetle to species level. Especially when dealing with a group so vast, that there may be more than 100 often very similar species in a single genus. Therefore not all of the images chosen here to illustrate the diversity of beetles in Australia are identified to species. They were chosen to represent beetles you are likely to see, or that represent a particular trait in the family they belong to. Families tell a lot about the lifestyle of the creatures that belong to them. For instance, all Leaf Beetles, family **Chrysomelidae**, really do eat leaves, and knowing what genus they belong to tells you something of the plants they are likely to be associated with, and whether they eat leaves from the edges or by holing or stripping the leaf surface. The most common genus in this family, *Paropsis*, has more than 70 species, with variability in their appearance across their ranges. But knowing they are this genus already tells you that they are probably associated with *Eucalyptus* and *Acacia* plants.

Bird books and butterfly books often have accurate distribution maps for each species. With beetles this is harder to accomplish, with vastly more species and less observers actively recording geodata. Several websites are amalgamating the geodata from museum specimens and observers all over the country, and the basis of this information has been used here to list the states they have been found in. It is a rough guide, but it at least can tell you which state has recorded the species as present somewhere within. This is why the wording is "it is recorded from...", which does not preclude that it may be found in other states, but our geodata logs have not yet recorded it from there. The numbers of species relate to Australia.

THE BEETLES

CARABIDAE – Ground Beetles (3,000 species)

These beetles are hunters, living mainly at ground level, although some hunt on trees. Both adults and larvae hunt other invertebrates from insects to worms. Most are active at night.

Gnathaphanus philippensis represents a very typical shape and dark colour that define the Ground Beetles. The genus has 16 very similar species all over Australia. 15mm.

The genus *Carenum* has more than 120 species all over Australia, many of which are desert specialists. They are characterised by the 'waist' in the middle of the body and are flightless. 15mm.

The Four-spot Ground Beetle, *Craspedophorus banksi*, is found in the east in Qld, NSW and Vic. 14mm.

Clivina biplagiata belongs to a genus with more than 340 Australian species, while the whole genus has more than 580 including those in Asia and Africa. Most are dark coloured, with some brown and others with coloured spots like here. Typical size is 10–12mm.

Dendrocellus smaragdinus is found in Qld, where it hunts on trees as well the ground. 12mm.

The flattened beetles in the genus *Trigonothops* live on the trunks of trees and hide under the bark during the day. Eighteen species are found all over Australia. About 10mm.

Beetles in the genus *Arthopterus* have an association with ants. The beetle larva lives inside ant nests, and has a secretion which stops the ants from seeing it as an enemy, while it devours the ant larvae. Adults also spend time with ants, but do not have the secretion, so instead have a toughened slippery body that is hard to attack. All states except Tas. 10mm.

Ophionea storeyi is in a genus of these very elongate, long-'necked' beetles which sometimes also hunt during the day. Twenty species are found in NT, Qld and NSW. 14mm.

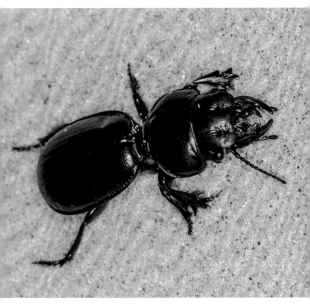

Scaraphites rotundipennis is one of seven species of moderately sized night hunters, characterised by the pinched 'waist' and large mandibles. This species is from Tas. Also found in Vic and NSW. 20mm.

27

Pamborus guerinii is a large nocturnal hunter specialising in snails and earthworms. The genus has 16 large species in Qld, NSW and Vic. 30mm.

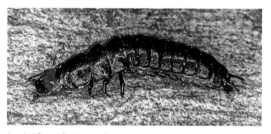

A typical Ground Beetle larva. They are roaming nocturnal hunters. Note how, unlike caterpillars, the body is quite armour-plated for the rough life it has on the forest floor. 20mm.

DYTISCIDAE – Diving Beetles (265 species)

A fully aquatic group, with larvae and adults adapted to hunt underwater. Both need to come to the surface to trap air, the adult doing so under the wing covers. When it is time to pupate the larvae comes out of the water. Like most aquatic insects, they prefer still waters, and recently many species have been discovered in deep underground aquifers.

Cybister tripunctatus is a very large species, found all over Australia, with other species in the genus found all the way to Europe. One of its common names is 'the toe biter' as it can and will bite feet standing in ponds. Otherwise it feeds on insects, tadpoles and fish. 26mm.

Sandracottus bakewelli is a northern Diving Beetle found in WA, NT and Qld.
Note the tiny edge of a trapped air bubble at the rear of its wing covers. 10mm.

Diving Beetle larvae have large mandibles and hunt insects and tadpoles. Here one is eating a bloodworm, the larva of a midge. Note the 'tail', which is a syphon – it touches the surface to draw in an air supply. 15mm.

GYRINIDAE – Whirligig Beetles (25 species)

These beetles are very noticeable as they swim madly in circles on the surface of ponds and slow creeks. They are hunters and scavengers on insects which fall onto the water. The ripples they and their prey cause are used like radar to pinpoint the prey location. They also have two sets of eyes, two looking down in the water for any enemies approaching, and two looking up in the air.

Macrogyrus elongatus is a typical Whirligig Beetle on the surface, showing the beginning of the ripples it is causing. Qld. 12mm.

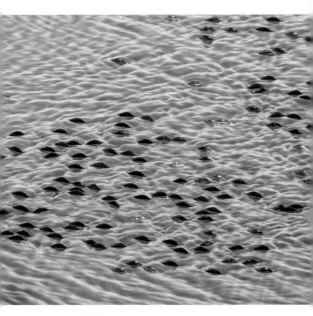

A mad swarm of Whirligig Beetles swimming helter-skelter on the surface of a slow stream.

Dineutus australis showing that Whirligigs can also hunt underwater, carrying a bubble of trapped air under their wing cases, like the Diving Beetles. 12mm.

HYDROPHILIDAE – Water Beetles (230 species)

A family of largely scavenging species, most of which live in or near water. Others are dung feeders. They store air along the bottom of their bodies, which are lined with a fine pubescence that allows the large air 'bubble' to cling; this is called plastron respiration. The larvae are often predators, and the pupa is attached to plants with a siphon to breathe.

Hydrobiomorpha sp, one of the larger Hydrophilids, showing the silver air pocket along the underside of its body. It is a scavenger in ponds. There are six similar species all over Australia. 24mm.

Spercheus sp is in a subfamily of rough-textured small beetles that live on stagnant ponds. These scavengers have the ability to walk on the surface and along the underside of the surface, with species in every Australian state. 3mm.

This unidentified species of Hydrophilid is in the group which feed on various native dung. This one is on wombat poo in Tas. 3mm.

HISTERIDAE – Hister Beetles (280 species)

Variable of habits. Some are predators, some scavengers and carrion eaters, while others live in ant nests. Their bodies are usually smooth and often shiny, for better movement through substrates such as flesh or dung.

Saprinus species belong to a genus of hunters. They live on carrion, where they do not eat the flesh but other insects, especially fly maggots. Some species of this group have been brought to Australia from Africa to help control bush flies. All over Australia. 5mm.

LEIODIDAE – Small Fungus Beetles (150 species)

These small to minute beetles are rarely seen as most live associated with fungi and leaf litter, and some live in ant nests. They feed mainly on fungi, and some decaying plant matter and are found all over Australia.

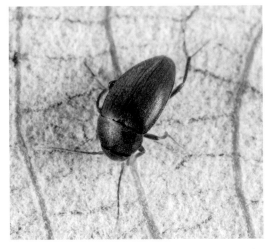

Nargiotes sp, is large by the standards of this family, at 5mm, and lives in leaf litter in the eastern states including Tas.

SILPHIDAE – Carrion or Burying Beetles (3 species)

These moderate-sized beetles are famous for the work they do burying carrion. They dig under the dead animal and make chambers filled with softened flesh, which they then feed to their larvae. This parental behaviour lasts for half the lifespan of the larvae.

Diamesus osculans is the largest of the Australian species. This one has just started working on a dead bandicoot. Found mainly in the eastern states and Tas. 30mm.

STAPHYLINIDAE – Rove Beetles (3,000 species)

A huge family, but with a characteristic that makes them fairly unique. The wing cases, or elytra, only cover the first few segments of the abdomen, even though folded inside are usually full-sized flying wings. Their bodies are very elongate, and the majority of species have dark colours. They are sometimes mistaken for earwigs, but lack the pincers at the back.

Actinus macleayi is a comparatively large and very showy Rove Beetle that lives a hunter lifestyle. It can sometimes be seen on carrion where it hunts the other visiting insects. Found mainly in Qld. 15mm.

The genus *Pinophilus* is very typical of Rove Beetles, having a skinny black body, short wing cases and being about 12mm long. This genus of 13 species is found in all states except WA. They should not be handled as they secrete an irritant chemical defence.

Species of the genus *Stenus* are extra skinny, with large eyes, sometimes a metallic sheen, and a habit of raising the abdomen. They are fast daytime hunters on vegetation, found all over except for Tas. 12mm.

The 60 species of the genus *Sepedophilus* have a body shape reminiscent of a silverfish, tapering at the rear. Found in all states except the NT. 10mm.

Scymbalium is a genus with about 15 species, with an elongate stout body, which, like *Pinophilus*, can secrete a foul irritant defensive chemical. Found in Qld, NSW, Vic and Tas. 14mm.

LUCANIDAE – Stag Beetles (110 species)

Stag Beetles are known for sometimes having extreme differences between the sexes, with males having very enlarged, antler-like mandibles. In some species they are used in dominance combat with other males, much like mammalian antlers. They are moderate to very large in size, with the majority coloured black, and some with stunning metallic colours.

Ryssonotus nebulosus is a common species in the eastern states of Qld, NSW and Vic, frequenting wetter coastal forests. 24mm.

This shiny male Stag Beetle is *Prosopocoilus torrensis*, a large inhabitant of tropical forests in north Qld and NT. 40mm.

Lamprima micardi belongs to a genus of very colourful species, with every hue possible with the light striking from different angles. Four very variable species are recorded from every state except NT.

The Golden Stag Beetle, *Lamprima aurata*, is one of the more exotic species found outside of the tropics, recorded from every state except NT. 20mm.

The King Stag Beetle, *Phalacrognathus muelleri*, is one of the largest beetles in Australia, with males up to 75mm. Its green to blue to copper sheen is truly amazing in the hand, which caused it to be very sought after by collectors around the world. Luckily it is not easy to find, and not threatened. Found only in the rainforests of north Qld.

PASSALIDAE – Passalid or Bess Beetles
(50 species)

A small family of elongate, flattened beetles which mainly live in and under rotting logs. Usually found in small family groups, apparently with some parental behaviour. Most species are black and of medium size, recorded in all states except WA.

Alaucocyclus sp is from the east coast, found in wetter forests where decaying logs provide a home. 28mm.

TROGIDAE – Hide Beetles (175 species)

Trogids are carrion feeders, specialising on older dry carcasses, and indeed are often found in the dry interior performing this work. This group is characterised by rows of tubercles along a hardened body, and a shovel-like head plate similar to that in Dung Beetles.

Most of the Australian species of carrion-feeding trogids belong to the genus *Omorgus*, which is found all over Australia. This one is from Broken Hill, NSW. 15mm.

GEOTRUPIDAE – Geotrupid Beetles (44 species)

The geotrupids were formerly classified as a separate family known as **Bolboceratidae**. They live in burrows, in which the larvae probably feed on fungus. This group is characterised by a domed body with antennae that end in a football-shaped club.

The fungus- and dung-feeding geotrupids are well characterised by this species of *Australobolbus*, with 44 species distributed in every state except Tas. 15mm.

HYBOSORIDAE – Scavenger Scarab Beetles (50 species)

Most of the family specialises in using older carcasses and dung for sustenance of the adults and larvae. They range from black to dark reddish, and have an antennal club similar to the Hide Beetles (Trogidae).

The domed bodies of the 30 species of *Liparochrus* are typical of this family. Found in NT, Qld, NSW and Vic. 12mm.

SCARABAEIDAE – Scarab Beetles, including Dung Beetles, Christmas Beetles and Chafers (3,500 species)

This huge family is divided into seven very distinct subfamilies. One characteristic they all share is the antennae being 'lamellate', meaning the last three segments are expanded into larger fan like segments. Shapes are often dome-like. Larvae are the very typical C-shaped grubs often dug up from the soil or detritus like compost.

Retulinae – Christmas Beetles (114 species)

Anoplognathus chloropyrus is found in Qld, NSW, Vic and SA. 25mm.

Most people are familiar with Christmas Beetles, which are often seen in large numbers over the summer. *Anoplognathus porosus* belongs to the largest genus, with 35 species all over Australia, usually associated with eucalypts. 25mm.

Xylonichus eucalypti is often seen in numbers on *Eucalyptus* trees in NSW, Vic and Tas. 24mm.

Calloodes atkinsoni is a large shiny species from Qld, in a genus of four other green species. 30mm.

Anolognathus aureus really is pure gold coloured. It is found in north Qld rainforests. 16mm.

Scarabaeinae and Aphodiinae – Dung Beetles (351 and 183 species)

The Scarabaeinae are the true Scarabs, made famous by ancient Egyptian mythology, paintings and sculptures. The dung-ball rolling habit of many African species was considered representative of the God Khepri rolling the sun across the sky each day. Australia does not have many such rolling species, but the habit of making tunnels

The genus *Onthophagus* is by far the largest group of Dung Beetles with more than 2,300 species worldwide and 203 species in Australia, six of which are introduced. *O. ferox* is found in WA and SA. The horns are a feature of the males. 16mm.

provisioned with dung, sometimes fungus, and even carrion, is universal. They have shovel-like heads and strong expanded front legs for digging. Native species are used to small dry marsupial dung and could not handle the large wet droppings of cows and other non-native animals. Therefore more than 40 Dung Beetle species have been imported from Africa and other areas to help dispose of this fly-breeding nuisance.

A member of the genus *Coptodactyla*, which has 15 species. Although native, they will also bury horse dung. Found in Qld and NT. 15mm.

Onitis alexis is one of the 45 or so species of Dung Beetles introduced into Australia by CSIRO to help bury cow dung to control bushflies and help the soils. 16mm.

The Aphodiinae subfamily is well represented by *Ataenius picinus*, which is part of a genus of 55 species, most of which are elongate and black, with striated wing cases and small size. They feed on dung and are found in Qld, NSW, Vic and Tas. 5mm.

Cetoniinae – Flower Chafers (141 species)

The Flower Chafers, sometimes called Rose Chafers, are a showy day-active group of beetles most often found on flowers. They share a somewhat rectangular body, flattened on top rather than domed, and are often brightly patterned.

Neorrhina (Polystigma) punctata is found in Qld, NSW, Vic and south WA. 15mm.

One of the commonest Flower Chafers is the Fiddler Beetle, *Eupoecila australasiae*, which is found on blossom in every state except Tas. 14mm.

Glycyphana brunnipes has a velvety textured body. Recorded from NSW, Qld and south WA. 12m.

The metallic *Ischiopsopha* sp is a tropical species from north Qld, NT and PNG. 24mm.

Melolonthinae – Chafers (1,250 species)

The Chafers are the largest Scarab group, with mainly nocturnal, plant-eating species, and others which frequent flowers during the day. Many are shades of brown, with a few genera of brightly coloured pollinator species.

A very common and typical Chafer species is *Sericesthis geminata*, which is a minor pest of some pastures because its larvas eat their roots. Found in Qld, NSW and Vic. 18mm.

Another pollinator group is the genus *Diphucephala*, with 68 often brightly metallic species, recorded from every state except NT. 8mm.

Phyllotocus apicalis is a very common pollinator species. It is in a genus with 28 very similar species found in every state except NT. 8mm.

The Grey-backed Cane Beetle, *Dermolepida albohirtum*, is a serious pest of sugar cane. To add insult to injury, it is also the reason why the Cane Toad was stupidly introduced to Australia in 1935. 25mm. Its larva is very typical for the whole Scarab family – a grub usually seen in this C-shaped pose.

67

Dynastinae – Rhinoceros and Elephant Beetles (192 species)

This subfamily includes species with sometimes very pronounced sexual dimorphism. Males often have small to large horns on the thorax and head. Some species can also stridulate to produce squeaking noises used in defence.

The Elephant Beetle, *Xylotrupes ulysses* is the largest and most famous Dynastine Beetle in Australia. It is often common along the coasts of Qld and northern NSW, and the males can sometimes be seen to congregate and fight each other for territory and females. 45mm.

Cyclocephala signaticollis is an accidental introduction from Argentina. It has spread to Qld, NSW, Vic and SA and is a pest of various grasses.

RHIPICERIDAE – Fan Beetles (15 species)

A small family of very distinctive beetles, with the males possessing fan-shaped antennae. It is also a mysterious group, as the life cycles of the Australian species are still unknown, with the larvae of most species not yet documented. There is a record of one larva being a parasite of cicada nymphs.

Typical Fan Beetle in the genus *Rhipicera*, found almost all over Australia. 20mm.

BUPRESTIDAE – Jewel Beetles (1,500 species)

This is an unmistakable family, with often very showy species active during the day, usually on flowers. The body is elongate, boat-shaped. Most of the larvae feed on wood, tunnelling through trunks, stems and roots.

One of the brightest Australian Jewel Beetles, the aptly named *Metaxymorpha gloriosa*, is found in Qld. 40mm.

Castiarina erythroptera in not wildly coloured, but instead protects itself by mimicking the colours of a poisonous beetle in the family Lycidae (see page 82). Found in Qld, NSW, Vic and SA. 16mm.

72

Castiarina macmillani belongs to the largest genus of Jewel Beetles, with more than 470 species. Patterns of similar transverse stripes in many species sometimes makes field ID difficult. This species is from WA. 18mm.

Castiarina bucolica stands out from other species in the genus thanks to its bold red striping. It is found in WA, often on the flowers of *Xanthorrhoea*, which is a magnet for Jewel Beetles and other pollinator insects. 18mm.

Stigmodera roei is another WA species. 25mm.

Cyrioides imperialis is a large species from Qld, NSW, Vic, Tas and SA. Its larvae feed on *Banksia*. 35mm.

Selagis caloptera is from the east, found in Qld, NSW and Vic, here feeding on *Eucalyptus* blossom, a favourite flower for many Jewel Beetles. 15mm.

Iridotaenia bellicosa is found in Qld. 25mm.

The genus *Castiarina* has 465 species in Australia, so this variable individual from WA is difficult to identify to the exact species. 16mm.

ELATERIDAE – Click Beetles (1,000 species)

These beetles are so named because they do literally click. It is part of an original startle mechanism. Between the thorax and abdomen is a ratchet-like locking mechanism which stores energy as the beetle flexes its body. When under attack, or just stuck upside-down, it releases the ratchet, suddenly noisily propelling it quite high, to help it to escape.

A typical shape of Click Beetles is this elongate body with a visible edge between the thorax and abdomen where the click mechanism is found. *Megapenthes* sp occur in every state but Tas. 18mm.

Cryptalaus species are broader and larger than most Click Beetles, and often have cryptic colours to blend with bark and other backdrops. There are 53 similar species all over Australia except Tas. 35mm.

The larvae of Click Beetles are sometimes called wireworms, with a hard and slippery body. Some are plant feeders and some may be predacious. 20mm.

LYCIDAE – Net-winged Beetles (300 species)

This beetle family is characterised by comparatively soft elytra, with faint net-like wing venation visible on most. The antennae of most have a slight serrated edge.

Porrostoma rhipidium. Until recently this genus was known as *Metiorrhynchus*. It contains about 105 species, most of which have strongly striated and cross-'veined' wings of the same deep brick red colour. They are poisonous to predators. Many other beetles, in other families, and even some moths, have evolved an almost exact copy of this colour. This mimicry helps to protect the edible mimics. Found all over Australia. 16mm.

Trichalus kershawi belongs to the other large genus of Lycids, with 36 species, most of which also share the brick red colour, though some have dark patterns overlaid. Genus found all over Australia, but *T. kershawi* only in Vic and Tas. 14mm.

LAMPYRIDAE – Fireflies (25 species)

The Fireflies are a small group of very recognisable beetles, with light-emitting organs on the last two segments of the abdomen in males, and just the one last segment in females. Their larvae are predators of snails and worms, and many also glow. In the mangrove forests of north Qld are species which synchronise their blinking lights, presenting a spectacular show.

Atyphella is the largest genus in Australia with 14 species found in Qld and NSW. Other species are found in damp forests in every state except SA. 12mm.

CANTHARIDAE – Soldier Beetles (200 species)

The Soldier Beetles, like the **Lycidae** family, have soft elytra, and bodies generally. Some species possess poisonous chemicals and are avoided by predators. Adults are commonly found at flowers, although many are also hunters of soft insects.

Chauliognathus is the largest genus with 32 species, many of which have similar mustard colours, such as *C. apicalis*. Found in every state. 16mm.

The Plague Soldier Beetle, *Chauliognathus lugubris*, reaches huge numbers in some summers, covering flowering trees and entering houses. It is best not to touch them as they exude a foul defensive fluid. Found mainly in the eastern states including Tas. 15mm.

DERMESTIDAE – Dermestid, Carpet and Museum Beetles (200 species)

Many Dermestid species are associated with natural fibres, skins and cadavers. Others eat grains and other stored products. Therefore some of the worst insect pests in the world belong to this family, such as the Khapra Beetle, Carpet Beetles and Museum Beetles.

Anthrenus contains species often found on flowers, but their larvae are also potential pests in urban environments, where they can live in the larder eating dry stored products, while they are also destroyers of insect and other museum collections. 5mm.

The hairy larva of the very destructive *Dermestes* sp feeds on everything from your carpet and woollens to dead bodies. Found everywhere. 12mm.

BOSTRICHIDAE – Auger Beetles, Shothole Borers (120 species)

A family with varied habits. The majority bore into damaged or dead trees, leaving tell-tale holes with frass, and a few are pests of stored grains such as rice. Adults are seldom seen, although some come to lights.

Bostrychopsis jesuita is a common borer species, preferring *Eucalyptus* and *Acacia* trees. Found all over Australia. 12mm.

LYMEXILIDAE – Ship-timber Beetles (15 species)

This is a seldom seen and small family, included here because at first glance they may not even be taken for beetles. They are cylindrical, very elongate and their larvae bore into hardwoods, including *Eucalyptus*.

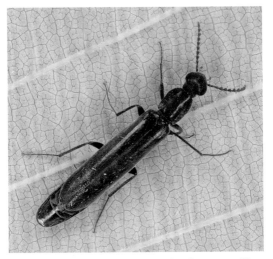

Australymexylon sp. This genus has been recorded from all states except NT. 25mm.

CLERIDAE – Checkered Beetles (400 species)

A varied family of mainly predacious beetles, often living in and on trees, and many are commonly found on flowers. A few species are pests, but there are also beneficial species which eat pest insects.

Stigmatium quadricostatum. This genus has 14 species of tree-based predators, which are seen in the open on bark. Found in Qld, NSW, Vic and SA. 14mm.

Phlogistus rufipes belongs to a genus of 48 species of mainly metallic beetles seen on many flowers, especially *Eucalyptus* and *Angophora* blossom. Recorded from every state but NT. 12mm.

Eleale pulcher is very common. It comes from a genus of more than 60 species with slightly flattened and angular bodies. Found on flowers in NSW and Vic. 16mm.

Many species of *Eleale* have sparkly metallic colours, ranging from green to deep blue and purple. The genus is found in every state. 18mm.

MELYRIDAE – Soft-winged Flower Beetles (350 species)

A family of small, soft-bodied beetles. Most species are hunters of small soft insects, and spend much time on flowers, feeding on the pollen while looking for prey. Some have bright warning colours, and several genera have short elytra, although with full flying wings tucked inside.

Dicranolaius bellulus is a very common species, seen on leaves and flowers where it hunts for small soft insects. It is in a genus of 80 similar species. Found in every state except NT. 8mm.

Another species of *Dicranolaius*. Note the greatly expanded first part of the antennae, which is a feature only of the males. This species is found in Qld. 8mm.

Carphurus armipennis. With 80 species, it is in the largest of several genera with very short elytra. This one's warning colours may indicate that it is distasteful to predators. Found in every state. 12mm.

NITIDULIDAE – Sap Beetles (400 species)

Sap Beetles can be found on flowers and on fruit, especially as it starts to rot. Some are dried-fruit pests and several species live with bees.

Species of the genus *Carpophilus*, with 36 species, are fruit feeders, especially favouring rotting fruit such as papaya (pictured). Recorded from every state except NT. 6mm.

Aethina concolor is common inside deep flowers where it feeds on pollen and nectar, often in groups. Found in the eastern states. 5mm.

SILVANIDAE – Silvanid Beetles (75 species)

Most species in this small family are very flattened and live under the bark of living and decaying trees. However, a few species are serious pests of stored products, such as this Saw-toothed Grain Beetle, *Oryzaephilus surinamensis*, which is an introduced pest of stored grains and nuts and fruits.

100

CUCUJIDAE – Flat Bark Beetles (8 species)

Members of this family of very flat beetles are seldom seen as they tend to live hidden under bark and in other crevices. However, *Platisus integricollis* is so distinctive that it deserved a mention. Found in the east and SA. 12mm.

EROTYLIDAE – Pleasing Fungus Beetles (120 species)

This is a mix of two previous families. The Erotylinae are true fungus beetles with both adults and larvae feeding on a variety of fungi, especially in decaying wood. The Languriinae are elongate shiny beetles, with almost nothing known about the habits of Australian species.

Thallis atricornis. Thallis is the most typical and frequently seen genus – it contains 17 species found in wet forests in every state, and especially Tas. 12mm.

Caenolanguria vulgaris represents a typical species on the other side of this family, the Languriinae beetles, which used to have the odd name of Lizard Beetles. Found in Qld and NSW. 14mm.

ENDOMYCHIDAE – Handsome Fungus Beetles (75 species)

The other main fungus-eating family are these usually flattened, rounded beetles, which often have a depressed 'ledge' along the outer edge of the elytra. Both adults and larvae are fungus- and mould-eaters in wet forests predominantly in the east. *Encymon immaculatus* is 10mm.

COCCINELLIDAE – Ladybirds (500 species)

Ladybirds need no introduction visually. Most have the same round domed shape, either with a shiny dome or covered in a fine velvety finish. The majority of species are hunters, especially of soft insects such as aphids, and so are gardeners' friends. However, a small part of the family has leaf-eating habits, especially of plants in the cucurbit family.

Harmonia (Leis) conformis is one of the most common and recognisable species, found in all states except NT. It frequents flowers and eats aphids. 8mm.

A typical *Harmonia* sp larva, munching on aphids. 10mm.

Epilachna sumbana is the Cucurbit Ladybird, with both adults and larvae feeding on a variety of plants, including many that are commonly grown in gardens. Recorded from Qld, NSW and Vic. 8mm.

107

In a departure from the usual Ladybird habits, *Illeis galbula* is a fungus eater.
Recorded from Qld, NSW, Vic, Tas and SA. 6mm.

The hard-working and voracious *Micraspis lineola* clearing an aphid infestation from a rose bud. Before spraying roses, check if nature is already providing a solution. Recorded from the top of WA across to Qld and NSW. 8mm.

Heterocaria delta is a species from Qld and NSW, seen here stripping the outer layer of a leaf. 8mm.

MORDELLIDAE – Pin-tail or Tumbling Flower Beetles, Fish Beetles (150 species)

These slippery, pointy-tailed, fast-moving beetles are often seen on flowers, and will jump off or fall off when approached. Many are pollen feeders, and the larvae have a variety of habits from predation to parasitism.

Mordella is a genus with an almost worldwide distribution, and almost half the Australian species of this family. Known larvae are mainly borers in dead wood. Recorded from every state except Tas. 12mm.

111

RHIPIPHORIDAE – Wedge-shaped Beetles (80 species)

Boat-shaped beetles similar to the Mordellids (page 111), but larger and with a more compact pointy tail end. Larvae are external parasites of various immature stages of beetles, wasps and cockroaches.

Trigonodera is a typical genus of the family. Seen on foliage and sometimes at lights. 18mm.

Macrosiagon novaehollandiae belongs to a genus that is found in every state. There are 14 species and some, like this one, are adapted to the deserts of the interior. 12mm.

TENEBRIONIDAE – Darkling Beetles
(1,700 species)

This large family has mainly dark-coloured species that are night active and at first appear similar in appearance to the Ground Beetles (see page 21). However, unlike the Ground Beetles, which are hunters, the Darkling Beetles are mainly plant eaters, especially of dead plant matter from rotting wood to decayed leaves, and many are fungivores. Many species have adapted well to the dry interior. Two groups recently added to this family are day active and sometimes seen on flowers.

Amarygmus morio is part of a genus with more than 50 species of these rotting-wood feeders, which hide under bark and logs during the day. Found all over Australia. 14mm.

Species of *Gonocephalum* are often desert-adapted, feeding on dry detritus as adults and roots as larvae. Found in every state except Tas. 10mm.

The Pie-dish Beetles are several genera of very flat desert-adapted species. They are night-active detritus feeders. Pictured is one of the 50 species of *Helea*, which are found inland in every state except Tas. 20mm.

Related to the Pie-dish Beetles, but without the extra-wide body flange, are more than 90 species of the genus *Pterohelaeus*. Many are also desert-adapted and they are found in every state. 18mm.

Chalcopteroides is a genus of more than 110 species of domed beetles, which often have a metallic sheen. They can be seen on tree trunks, under bark or logs, and most are night-active. Found in every state. 12mm.

Ecnolagria rufescens. This day-active group, the Lagriinae, was recently absorbed from its own family. Most species are from brown to dark blue in colour and slightly pubescent. They roam on foliage and are found in every state. 10mm.

Another family recently added to the Darkling Beetles is the now subfamily Alleculinae. Most are day-active. *Euomma lateralis* is from all states except NT and Tas. 14mm.

The subfamily Alleculinae has some wildly metallic species in the genus *Lepturidea* (46 species once known as *Aethyssius*). They can be seen on flowers in spring and summer, and are found in every state except Tas. 15mm.

The genus *Promethis* has some large, flat species living in old logs and found roaming at night. The 14 species are found only in the east, including Tas. 24mm.

Cyphaleus planus is a large, handsome metallic beetle among 29 other species in the genus, found mainly in the east and into SA. It is a nocturnal detritus feeder. 25mm.

Adelium tenebrioides is in a genus with 92 species recorded from every state. They can be found under stones, bark, logs or leaf litter, and are mainly nocturnal detritus feeders. 14mm.

OEDEMERIDAE – False Blister Beetles
(100 species)

This small family has day-active beetles, with the thorax narrower than the abdomen, prominent eyes and antennae that point straight forward. Adults frequent flowers, and larvae feed in rotting wood and other plant matter. *Sessinia nigronotata* is in a genus with 20 species, some of which look much like Lycid beetles (see page 82). 15mm.

MELOIDAE – Oil Beetles, Blister Beetles (100 species)

Blister Beetles are famous for some species being highly poisonous if ingested by a predator. They were even used in some ancient court murders, through being added to wine as a poison. They were then called 'Spanish Fly'. The chemical, called cantharidin, blisters the skin, hence the name. Their larvae are parasites inside bee nests, and adults are commonly seen on flowers.

Australozonitis lutea is in the typical Blister Beetle genus with more than 70 species found all over, although with less in WA. They were previously placed in the genus *Zonitis*, some of which have bright warning colours. 16mm.

Palaestra foveicollis is mimicking the warning colours sported by many Lycid Beetles (see page 82), and other mimics of that general red-brick colour signifying 'danger'. Found in NSW. 15mm.

ANTHICIDAE – Ant Beetles (250 species)

Small beetles, many of which appear to have a 'waist' and 'neck', giving them a superficial resemblance to the ant body shape. Adults are often seen at flowers, and larvae live in damp detritus, such as that which accumulates on the edge of water bodies.

Some Ant Beetles have strong colours, such as *Lemodes* species. *L. coccinea*, illustrated here, is covered in fine red velvet. Found in eastern states and SA. 5mm.

Pseudocyclodinus sp is quite ant-like in shape. It is recorded from the south, across from WA to SA, NSW, Vic and Tas. 5mm.

CERAMBYCIDAE – Longicorn Beetles, Longhorn Beetles (1,500 species)

This very distinctive family is characterised by long antennae, sometimes two or more times the length of the body. They were a favourite with collectors. Alfred Russel Wallace, the co-father of the theory of evolution, found literally thousands in his South-East Asian travels, and seeing their distribution along the islands helped him to ask the right questions. They are all herbivores, and adults are among important pollinators, often seen on blossoms, such as *Eucalyptus*. The larvae burrow in wood, for a year or more, and formed a food item for Aboriginal people. They are not *the* witjuti grub (which are species of Goat Moths), but very similar by virtue of the same lifestyle.

Rhytiphora nigrovirens belongs to a genus recently amalgamated with others, so it now has more than 200 species. In older books this one was named *Platymopsis nigrovirens*. It is found all along the east coast of mainland Australia. 20mm.

One the largest species is the magnificent *Batocera boisduvali*. Found in Qld and north NSW rainforests, where its larvae bore in fig trees. As in many species, the male (pictured) has longer antennae than the female. 60mm.

Rhytiphora pardalis (previously known as *Penthea pardalis*) is a common species seen on *Acacia* bushes in all states except Tas. 24mm.

Xixuthrus microcerus is Australia's largest Longicorn, with formidable jaws used to dig into the bark of trees. Native only to north Qld. 75mm.

Coptocercus trimaculatus belongs to a genus with 39 species, split from the once larger genus *Phoracantha*. Many similar species are associated with eucalypts all over Australia. 20mm.

This species of *Psilomorpha* is found in Qld, NSW and Vic. It was once in the genus *Aphiorhynchus*. 12mm.

Chlorophorus curtisi was once classified in the genus *Clytus*, which has an almost worldwide distribution. They have relatively short antennae and are day active. Recorded from Qld and NSW. 12mm.

135

Scoleobrotus westwoodii belongs to a genus of 40 species, many associated with *Banksia*, though the larvae breed in *Eucalyptus*. They have been recorded from every state. 18mm.

Sceleocantha pilosicollis. The species name means 'hairy', and this large, stout beetle does have a downy underside. From WA. 35mm.

Strongylurus thoracicus is a hairy species, recorded from Qld, NSW and Vic. Its larvae are associated with *Pittosporum* plants. 26mm.

Syllitus rectus is part of a genus of 27 species, with small and very thin beetles often seen in native flowers. They are associated with **Myrtaceae** plants, and some with *Acacia*. Recorded from Qld, NSW, Vic, Tas and SA. 10mm.

Aridaeus thoracicus is commonly seen on blossom, especially *Angophora* and *Eucalyptus*. Its colour pattern is a general wasp-mimic warning. Recorded from Qld, NSW, Vic and south WA. 16mm.

Stenoderus suturalis is another small pollinator species. It is recorded from flowers in every state except NT. 10mm.

This stout-bodied Longicorn is *Rhytiphora albospilota*, meaning 'white spotted'. It has been recorded from Qld, NSW and Vic. 26mm.

Males of *Piesarthrius marginellus* have ornate antennae. They breed in *Acacia* and are found in the east, in Qld, NSW and Vic. 15mm.

Hesthesis assimilis. A number of Longicorn genera are general wasp mimics, helping their survival as they live an active and visible life on flowers. *Hesthesis* has 14 species. Note the very short elytra, which nevertheless house full-size flying wings. Their larvae are associated with *Eucalyptus* and *Leptospermum.* 18mm.

143

A less common mimicry among Longicorns is to imitate ants, such as this tiny *Ochyra coarctata*. It also has short elytra, but full flying wings inside. Often seen on flowers in NSW, Vic and Tas. 9mm.

One of the larger species, *Agrianome spinicollis* is recorded from Qld, NSW and Vic. 50mm.

A typical Longicorn larvae, found in the tunnel it digs for up to several years. As the wood gets older and drier, the growth cycle slows down, so that there are records of Longicorns emerging from furniture after decades, with a record of 40 years since the tree was felled!

145

CHRYSOMELIDAE – Leaf Beetles (3,500 species)

One of the largest beetle families, and probably the most noticeable, as most are exposed diurnal leaf feeders. Even the larvae share the same resource, something rare among beetles. There are many subfamilies with general body shapes within. The largest group are the Chrysomelinae, where most have a domed appearance. When living an exposed life, it helps to not be visible for too long, so larval cycles are very fast, measured in weeks.

Chrysomelinae

Paropsis maculata belongs to the 70-strong genus of perhaps the most commonly seen Leaf Beetles. All have this domed body shape and feed openly on top of leaves. Recorded from Qld, NSW and Vic. 10mm.

Paropsis tasmanica is found in Vic and Tas, on young eucalypt leaves. 10mm.

Paropsis obsoleta is found in Qld, NSW, Vic and SA. 10mm.

Paropsisterna sexpustulata belongs to a genus very similar to *Paropsis*, with more than 120 species, and often a more shiny body than *Paropsis*. This one is recorded from Qld, NSW and Vic. 12mm.

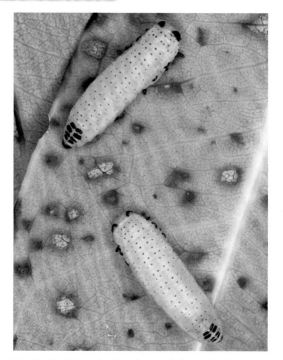

Typical Leaf Beetle larvae, here *Paropsisterna* sp, feeding openly on leaves.
15mm.

This very common species is *Dicranosterna immaculata*, in a genus of 28 species also similar to *Paropsis*. Recorded from Qld, NSW, Vic, Tas and SA. 12mm.

Phyllocharis cyanicornis has very bold colours, and is possibly distasteful to predators. Recorded from Qld, NSW and Vic. 12mm.

A very common Leaf Beetle, *Calomela bartoni*, recorded from *Acacia* bushes in Qld, NSW and Vic, although actually more widespread. The genus has 47 similar species. 10mm.

Calomela pallida is recorded from Qld, NSW, Vic and NT. 10mm.

Cassidinae

Hispellinus multispinosus, as the name suggests, is very spiny. It is often seen on grasses and occurs in every state. 8mm.

The Tortoise Beetles are remarkable for having this tortoise-like shield elytra, which extends beyond the body underneath, and in most, has a see-through edge. *Aspidimorpha westwoodi* is found in Qld and NSW. 10mm.

Cassida diomma is a Tortoise Beetle found across the north of WA, NT and most of Qld. 8mm.

Eumolpinae

The handsome *Colasposoma sellatum* represents a typical shape for members of the subfamily Eumolpinae. It is recorded from NT and north Qld. 12mm.

The genus *Geloptera* has some common species in every state. 8mm.

Cryptocephalinae

The genus *Aporocera* has species with a very typical shape for the whole
subfamily of Cryptocephalinae. The genus, with more than 150 species, is
recorded from every state, but is more prevalent in the south-east and Tas. 8mm.

Aporocera erosa is another species of this large genus which has species of many colours, but consistent shape. Recorded from NSW, Vic and Tas. 8mm.

Galerucinae

Oides fryi lives mainly on the kangaroo vine, *Cissus* sp, in the eastern states. 10mm.

Oides dosrosignata is recorded from Qld and NSW. 10mm.

Monolepta oculata is part of a genus that contains more than 700 species worldwide. They are known as Skeletonising Leaf Beetles as many eat the outer 'coat' of leaves, leaving behind the ribs, and others eat holes into the leaf rather than chew from the edge. Several species are pests. Found in every state. 6mm.

CURCULIONIDAE – Weevils (8,000 species)

The Weevils are the most speciated insects on the planet, characterised by their mouthparts protruding on a structure called a rostrum, which can be short or even longer than the body. Their antennae are bent in the middle, known as elbowed. Most adults feed on plants, including seeds, which means that some species are pests of our stored products. Larvae mainly burrow in wood and roots, and some feed on fungi.

The Botany Bay Diamond Weevil, *Chrysolophus spectabilis*, is our most famous weevil, described by Joseph Banks when on the Cook expedition of 1770. Found on *Acacia*, they have been recorded from Qld, NSW, Vic and SA. 16mm.

Orthorthinus cylindrirostris is a common species often seen on young eucalypts, although it has also taken to bothering grape vines. Recorded from every state. 16mm.

This large weevil, *Iphthimorhinus australasiae*, is associated with palms and *Pandanus* plants. Recorded from north Qld, north NT and New Guinea. 35mm.

Leptopius quadridens belongs to a widespread and common genus of more than 80 species found in every state, and often associated with *Acacia*. 15mm.

The genus *Gonipterus* has 21 similar-looking species and is found in every state.
It is usually seen on young eucalypts. 10mm.

Pantorhytes stanleyanus, the Clown Weevil, belongs to a genus of more than 70 species that are also found in New Guinea and South-East Asia, where some are wildly coloured. In Australia found only in north Qld. 12mm.

A typical weevil larva and pupa (right), here belonging to the Mango Weevil, *Sternochetus frigidus*.

169

While there are some pest species among the weevils, there are also some beneficials. *Cyrtobagous salviniae* feeds on the introduced giant *Salvinia* water weed, which seriously infested Australian waterways, until it was introduced and successfully controlled it in one year. 8mm.

Xyleborus perforans belongs to a very atypical Weevil subfamily, the Scolytinae, with tiny beetles called Bark Beetles and Pinhole Borers. They make intricately patterned tunnels in the sap wood, just under the bark of trees. As such some, like this species, are pests. It is originally from Asia but has spread around the world. 5mm.

Catasarcus cardo is in a desert-adapted genus with 32 widely distributed species, but this one is found only in WA. 12mm.

Pinhole Borers, or Ambrosia Beetles, subfamily Platypodinae, are tiny cylindrical Weevils adapted to tunnelling in wood. They 'seed' the tunnels with *Ambrosia* fungus, and this is their farmed food. Their tiny perfectly round holes are often seen under bark. *Platypus australis* is found in eastern states including Tas. 6mm.

Several groups of Weevil species are very heavily armoured and live on the ground, especially in arid zones. They live long slow, mainly nocturnal lives, and some species do not fly. Here a *Gagatophorus* sp (previously named *Macramycterus*) from WA. 20mm.

Meriphus is a genus of 11 species with long rostrums and day-active flower-feeding habits. Recorded from all states except NT. 10mm.

This very flat Weevil is adapted for life under bark. *Cossonus praeustus* is from Tas, and the 23 other species in this genus are found in the eastern states. 10mm.

Sitophilus orizae, the Rice Weevil, is part of a genus of pest species that attack many grains, seeds and other stored products around the world. 4mm.

Haplonyx species have longer front legs, and some of its 60 species are sometimes found in this signature branch-hugging pose. Found in every state. 8mm.

BRENTIDAE – Straight-snouted Weevils (250 species)

These often very skinny and elongate weevils also differ from true weevils but not having the 'elbowed' antennae. Their larvae are borers in wood, especially in newly fallen trees.

Baryrhynchus lineicollis is one of the larger species, found in Qld and PNG. This is a male with its long rostrum. Female brentids have short rostrums, or just normal strong mandibles. 18mm.

178

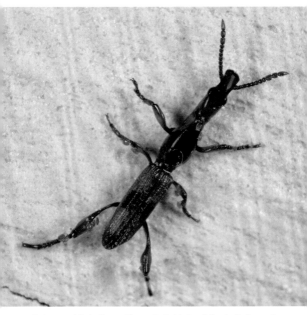

Cyphagogus delicatus is very skinny and cylindrical, as it lives inside the small wood tunnels made by Ambrosia Beetles (see page 172). Recorded from Qld, NSW, Vic and Tas. 10mm.

Brentids in general are not pests, but *Cylas formicarius*, accidentally introduced from Asia, is a pest of sweet potato. Recorded from Qld, NSW, Vic and SA. 10mm.

The Apioninae used to be a classified as family of its own, but these tiny, bulbous-shaped beetles are now incorporated in the Brentids. This is *Apion argutulum*, one of 33 similar species found all over Australia. 6mm.

ATTELABIDAE – Leaf-rolling Weevils (100 species)

The genus *Euops* is typical of these beetles. Shown here are the male, with the long front legs, and the female, which is cooperating to cut a leaf in a way to create a roll. An egg is laid in a slit in the leaf, and the larva lives inside the roll. Twenty-eight species of *Euops* live in Qld, NSW, Vic and SA. 10mm.

ANTHRIBIDAE – Fungus Weevils (200 species)

These weevils have the rostrum absent or short and broad, and straight antennae that are sometimes very long. They are associated mainly with fungi, with the larvae mainly found in soft decaying wood.

Ozotomerus sp mimicking bird droppings. The cylindrical shape is typical of the family. Recorded from wet forests in Qld and NT. 12mm.

The genus *Taburnus* shows the typical short broad rostrum of this family. Four species are recorded from Qld, NSW, Vic and WA. 12mm.

BELIDAE – Belid Weevils (200 species)

The majority of species in this family are found in Australia. Many have a relationship with *Acacia*, with larvae boring into the wood, and the day-active adults seen on the leaves.

Rhinotia suturalis on *Acacia*. With a long, cylindrical, pointed rear-end this species is typical of the whole family. The genus has 78 similar species, which are found in every state. 16mm.

Rhinotia haemoptera is a mimic of the distasteful species of the family **Lycidae** (see page 82). Recorded from Qld, NSW, Vic and SA. 18mm.

GLOSSARY

ABDOMEN The rear of the three body divisions of an insect, containing most of the internal organs and the reproductive parts

COMPLETE LIFE CYCLE The growth cycle where the young (the larvae) have a different form from the adult, and undergo a pupal stage to become the adult.

ELYTRA The hardened forewings that protect the membranous hindwings in beetles (Coleoptera) and are not used in flight.

EXOSKELETON The tough, jointed outer covering or skeleton of insects and other arthropods. It is made of chitin; and as it does not grow it has to be shed (moulted)

MANDIBLES The upper, chewing pair of mouthparts (jaws) of insects, sometimes modified into other shapes. They work sideways.

PUPA (pl. PUPAE) The usually inactive stage between larva and adult, found in insects with a COMPLETE LIFE CYCLE

SCLEROTISED. Hardened (or armoured) like the ELYTRA of a beetle, compared to the soft tissue of, for example, caterpillars.

THORAX The middle of the three major body divisions of an insect between head and ABDOMEN. The legs and wings are appendages of the thorax.

FURTHER READING

ONLINE RESOURCES

Australian Museum:
australian.museum/learn/animals/insects/beetles-order-coleoptera

Brisbane Insects has IDs for many east-coast species:
brisbaneinsects.com/brisbane_beetles/index.html

For great pictures of beetles from all over the world:
flickr.com/groups/beetles

Atlas of Living Australia is a huge resource for IDs and distributions. It is updated daily:
ala.org.au

A great citizen-science site for recording wildlife sightings, including lots of beetles:
inaturalist.ala.org.au

BOOKS and EBOOKS

Hangay, G, and de Keyzer, R (2017). *A Guide to Stag Beetles of Australia*. CSIRO.

Hangay, G, and Zborowski, P (2010). *A Guide to the Beetles of Australia*. CSIRO.

Slipinski, A, and Lawrence, J (2013). *Australian Beetles*, Volume 1. CSIRO.

Slipinski, A, and Lawrence, J (2019). *Australian Beetles*, Volume 2. CSIRO.

Zborowski, P, and Storey, R (2017). *A Field Guide to Insects in Australia*, Fourth Edition. Reed New Holland.

Zborowski, P (2019). *Insects of the World*. Reed New Holland.

INDEX

A

Actinus macleayi 41
Adelium tenebrioides 123
Adephaga 15
Aethina concolor 99
Aethyssius 120
Agrianome spinicollis 145
Alaucocyclus 50
Alleculinae 119–120
Amarygmus morio 114
Ambrosia Beetles 172, 179
Anolognathus aureus 57
Anoplognathus chloropyrus 54
Anoplognathus porosus 55
Ant Beetles 127
Anthicidae 127
Anthrenus 87
Anthribidae 182
Aphodiinae 58, 60
Aphiorhynchus 134
Apion argutulum 180
Apioninae 180
Aporocera erosa 161
Archostemata 15
Aridaeus thoracicus 140
Aspidimorpha westwoodi 156
Ataenius picinus 60
Arthopterus 25
Attelabidae 181
Atyphella 84
Auger Beetles 89

Australobolbus 52
Australozonitis lutea 125
Australymexylon 90

B

Bark Beetles 101, 170
Baryrhynchus lineicollis 178
Batocera 8, 130
Batocera boisduvali 130
Belid weevils 184
Belidae 184
Blister Beetles 124–125
Bostrichidae 89
Bostrychopsis jesuita 89
Botany bay diamond
    weevil 164
Brentidae 178
Buprestidae 71
Burying Beetles 40

C

Caenolanguria vulgaris 103
Callirhipidae 14
Calloodes atkinsoni 57
Calomela bartoni 153
Calomela pallida 154
Cantharidae 85
Carabidae 17, 21
Carenum 22
Carpet Beetles 87
Carphurus armipennis 97
Carpophilus 98
Cassida diomma 157
Castiarina bucolica 74

Castiarina erythroptera 72
Castiarina macmillani 73
Catasarcus cardo 171
Cerambycidae 129
Cetoniinae 12, 16, 61
Chafers 16, 54, 61–62, 65
Chalcopteroides 117
Chauliognathus lugubris 86
Checkered Beetles 91
Chlorophorus curtisi 135
Christmas Beetles 54–55
Chrysolophus spectabilis 164
Chrysomelidae 11, 13,
    15, 17–18, 146
Chrysomelinae 146
Cleridae 91
Click Beetles 79–81
Clivina biplagiata 23
Clytus 135
Coccinellidae 16, 105
Colasposoma sellatum 158
Coptocercus trimaculatus 133
Coptodactyla 59
Cossonus praeustus 175
Craspedophorus banksi 23
Cryptalaus 80
Cryptocephalinae 160
Cucujidae 101
Cucurbit ladybird 107
Curculionidae 17, 164
Cybister tripunctatus 29

Cyclocephala signaticollis 69
Cylas formicarius 180
Cyphagogus delicatus 179
Cyphaleus planus 122
Cyrioides imperialis 76
Cyrtobagous salviniae 170

D
Darkling Beetles 12, 114, 119
Dendrocellus smaragdinus 24
Dermestes 88
Dermestidae 87
Dermolepida albohirtum 67
Diamesus osculans 40
Dicranolaius bellulus 95
Dicranosterna immaculata 151
Dineutus australis 34
Diphucephala 66
Diving Beetles 29–31, 34
Dung Beetles 51, 54, 58–60
Dynastinae 68
Dytiscidae 29

E
Ecnolagria rufescens 118
Elateridae 79
Eleale pulcher 93
Elephant Beetles 68
elytra 6–7, 41, 82, 85, 95, 97, 104, 143–144, 156, 186

Encymon immaculatus 104
Endomychidae 104
Epilachna sumbana 107
Erotylidae 102
Erotylinae 102
Eumolpinae 158
Euops 181
Eupoecila australasiae 62
exoskeleton 10, 186

F
Fan Beetles 70
False Blister Beetles 124
Fiddler Beetle 62
Fireflies 84
Fish Beetles 111
Flat Bark Beetles 101
Flower Chafers 61–62
Fungus Weevils 182

G
Gagatophorus 173
Geloptera 159
Geotrupidae 52
Glycyphana brunnipes 63
Gnathaphanus philippensis 21
Gonipterus 168
Gonocephalum 115
Grey-backed Cane Beetles 67
Ground Beetles 9, 17, 21, 23, 28, 114
Gyrinidae 32

H
Handsome Fungus

Beetles 104
Haplonyx 177
Harmonia conformis 16
Helea 116
Hesthesis assimilis 143
Heterocaria delta 110
Hide Beetles 51, 53
Hispellinus multispinosus 155
Histeridae 38
Hister Beetles 38
Hybosoridae 53
Hydrobiomorpha 35
Hydrophilidae 35

I
Illeis galbula 108
Iphthimorhinus australasiae 166
Iridotaenia bellicosa 77
Ischiopsopha 64

J
Jewel Beetles 71, 73–74, 76

K
King Stag Beetle 49

L
Ladybirds 15–16, 105
Lamprima aurata 48
Lamprima micardi 47
Lampyridae 84
Languriinae 102–103
larvae 10–13, 21, 25, 29, 31, 35, 40, 51, 53–54,

INDEX

70–71, 76, 81, 84, 87, 90, 102, 104, 106–107, 111–112, 115, 124–125, 127, 129–130, 136, 138, 143, 145–146, 150, 164, 178, 182, 184, 186

Leaf Beetles 9, 11, 13, 15, 17, 146, 150, 153, 163
Leptopius quadridens 167
Lepturidea 120
Longhorn Beetles 129
Longicorn Beetle 8, 9, 129
Lymexilidae 90
Liparochrus 53
Leiodidae 39
Lucanidae 45
Lycidae 72, 82, 85, 185

M

Macramycterus 173
Macrogyrus 32
Macrosiagon novaehollandiae 113
Mecynognathus daemeli 9
Megapenthes 79
Meloidae 125
Melolonthinae 65
Melyridae 95
Meriphus 174
Metaxymorpha gloriosa 71
Micraspis lineola 109
Monolepta oculata 163
Mordella 111
Mordellidae 111
Museum Beetles 87

Myxophaga 15

N

Nargiotes 39
Net-winged Beetles 82
Nitidulidae 98

O

Ochyra coarctata 144
Oedemeridae 2
Oides dosrosignata 162
Oides fryi 162
Oil Beetles 125
Omorgus 51
Onitis alexis 60
Onthophagus 58
Ophionea storeyi 26
Orthorhinus cylindrirostris 165
Oryzaephilus surinamensis 100
Ozotomerus 182

P

Palaestra foveicollis 126
Pamborus guerini 28
Pantorhytes stanleyanus 169
Paropsis 11, 18, 146–149, 151
Paropsis maculata 146
Paropsis obsoleta 148
Paropsis tasmanica 147
Paropsisterna sexpustulata 149
Passalidae 50

Pentatomidae 7
Penthea pardalis 131
Phlogistus rufipes 92
Phalacrognathus muelleri 49
Phoracantha 133
Phyllocharis cyanicornis 152
Phyllotocus apicalis 66
Pie-dish Beetles 116
Piesarthrius marginellus 142
Pinhole borers 170, 172
Pinophilus 42, 44
Plague Soldier Beetle 86
Platisus integricollis 101
Platypodinae 172
Platypus australis 172
Pleasing Fungus Beetles 102
Polyphaga 15
Porrostoma rhipidium 82
Promethis 121
Prosopocoilus torrensis 46
Pseudocyclodinus 128
Psilomorpha 134
Pterohelaeus 116
pupae 186

R

Rhinotia haemoptera 185
Rhinotia suturalis 184
Rhipicera 70
Rhipiceridae 70
Rhipiphoridae 6, 112

Rhytiphora albospilota 141
Rhytiphora nigrovirens 129
Rhytiphora pardalis 131
Rice Weevil 176
Rove Beetles 41–42
Ryssonotus nebulosus 45

S
Sandracottus bakewelli 30
Sap Beetles 98
Saprinus 38
Saw-toothed Grain
   Beetle 100
Scarabaeidae 10, 12,
   16–17, 54
Scarabaeinae 58
*Scaraphites
   rotundipennis* 27
Scavenger Scarab
   Beetles 53
*Sceleocantha
   pilosicollis* 137
*Scoleobrotus
   westwoodii* 136
Scymbalium 44
Selagis caloptera 76

Sepedophilus 44
Sericesthis geminata 65
Sessinia nigronotata 124
Silphidae 40
Silvanid Beetles 100
Silvanidae 100
Sitophilus orizae 176
Soft-winged Flower
   Beetles 95
Soldier Beetles 85, 86
Spanish Fly 125
Spercheus 36
Stag Beetle 13, 45, 46,
   48–49
Stenoderus suturalis 140
Stenus 43
Sternochetus frigidus 169
Stigmodera roei 75
Strongylurus thoracicus 138
Syllitus rectus 139

T
Taburnus 183
Tenebrio molitor 12
Tenebrionidae 12, 114
Thallis atricornis 102

Tortoise Beetles 156, 157
Trichalus kershawi 83
Trigonodera 112
Trigonothops 24
Trogidae 51, 53
Tumbling Flower
   Beetles 111

W
Wedge-shaped Beetles 112
Weevils 10, 17, 164, 170,
   172, 178, 181–182, 184
Whirligig Beetles 32–33
wings 6–7, 10, 41, 82, 95,
   143–144, 186
Wireworms 81

X
Xixuthrus microcerus 132
Xyleborus perforans 170
Xylonichus eucalypti 56
Xylotrupes ulysses 68

Z
Zonitis 125

OTHER TITLES IN THE REED CONCISE GUIDES SERIES:

Reed Concise Guide: Animals of Australia
Ken Stepnell
ISBN 978 1 92151 754 9

Reed Concise Guide: Birds of Australia
Ken Stepnell
ISBN 978 1 92151 753 2

Reed Concise Guide: Butterflies of Australia
Paul Zborowski
ISBN 978 1 92554 694 1

Reed Concise Guide: Frogs of Australia
Marion Anstis
ISBN 978 1 92151 790 7

Reed Concise Guide: Insects of Australia
Paul Zborowski
ISBN 978 1 92554 644 6

Reed Concise Guide: Snakes of Australia
Gerry Swan
ISBN 978 1 92151 789 1

Reed Concise Guide: Spiders of Australia
Volker W Framenau and Melissa L Thomas
ISBN 978 1 92554 603 3

Reed Concise Guide: Trees of Australia
David L Jones
ISBN 978 1 92554 688 0

Reed Concise Guide: Wild Flowers of Australia
Ken Stepnell
ISBN 978 1 92151 755 6

OTHER BOOKS ON INSECTS FROM REED NEW HOLLAND INCLUDE:

Insects of the World
Paul Zborowski
ISBN 978 1 92554 609 5

A Field Guide to Insects in Australia
(4th edition)
Paul Zborowski and Ross Storey
ISBN 978 1 92554 607 1

World's Weirdest Bugs
Paul Zborowski
ISBN 978 1 92158 036 9

For details of these books and hundreds of other Natural History titles see:
www.newhollandpublishers.com
and follow ReedNewHolland on Facebook and Instagram